Read Along

워크북

> 이 책은 메인북인 **워크북**과
> 별책인 **스토리북**, 전 2권으로
> 분리하여 볼 수 있습니다.
> 스토리북을 통해 영화의 내용을
> 영어로 가볍게 읽고 워크북으로
> 알차게 학습해 보세요 "

워크북의 구성

스토리북을 네 개의 파트로 나누어 다양한 액티비티를 담았습니다.
워크북에 담긴 즐거운 활동을 통해 영어 실력을 키워 보세요!

＜ Fun Fact

각 파트마다 영화 내용과 관련된 흥미로운 이야기를 수록하여,
스토리북을 보다 알차게 읽을 수 있도록 구성했습니다.
다양한 주제로 쓰여진 흥미로운 글을 통해 영어 읽기의 재미를
느껴 보세요.

Vocabulary ＞

스토리북 본문에서 볼드로 표시된 주요 단어들을
각 파트별로 정리했습니다. 그림과 예문이 함께
나와 있어 단어의 뜻을 쉽게 이해할 수 있습니다.

＜ Learning activities

다채로운 학습 액티비티로 나만의 영어 실력을
쌓아 보세요. 단어, 표현, 그리고 내용 이해까지
확실하게 짚어 줍니다.

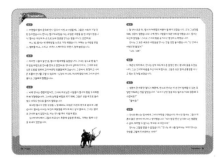

Review

워크북에 수록된 스티커를 이용하여 이야기 지도와 좋아하는 캐릭터에 대한 소개까지 완성해 보세요! 자연스럽게 이야기를 다시 확인하고 정리할 수 있습니다.

Translation

스토리북의 내용이 완전히 이해되지 않는다면? 워크북 속 친절한 한국어 번역을 확인해 보세요! 최대한 직역에 가깝게 번역되어 원서 읽기의 길잡이가 되어 줍니다.

오디오북

듣기 훈련용   따라 읽기용

QR코드를 인식하여 '듣기 훈련용 오디오북'과 '따라 읽기용 오디오북'의 두 가지 오디오북을 들어 보세요! '듣기 훈련용 오디오북'은 정식 오디오북으로 오리지널 캐릭터 목소리와 재미있는 효과음이 곁들여져 원서의 내용을 실감나게 듣고 즐길 수 있습니다. '따라 읽기용 오디오북'은 초보 영어 학습자들을 위해 조금 더 천천히 녹음한 오디오북으로 학습용으로 사용하기에 유용할 것입니다.

2 스토리북의 구성

별책으로 분리하여 더욱 가볍게 읽을 수 있는 스토리북! 간결한 이야기와 함께 영화 속 장면과 대사가 담겨 있어 영화의 재미와 감동을 다시 한 번 느낄 수 있습니다. 이야기에 나오는 주요 단어를 볼드로 강조하여, 문맥 속의 단어들을 더 확실히 인지하도록 도와줍니다.

Contents

Part 1
- 워크북 · · · · · · · · · · · · · 06~15
- 스토리북 · · · · · · · · · · · · 02~09

Part 2
- 워크북 · · · · · · · · · · · · · 16~25
- 스토리북 · · · · · · · · · · · · 10~17

Listen and Read Along 1
- 워크북 · · · · · · · · · · · · · 26~27
- 스토리북 · · · · · · · · · · · · 02~17

Part 3
- 워크북 · · · · · · · · · · · · · 28~37
- 스토리북 · · · · · · · · · · · · 18~25

Part 4

· 워크북 ················· 38~47

· 스토리북 ············· 26~32

Listen and Read Along 2

· 워크북 ················· 48~49

· 스토리북 ············· 18~32

Story Map

· 워크북 ················· 50~51

Character Chart

· 워크북 ················· 52

❆ Translation ··············· 53~61

❆ Answer ················· 62~63

· Part ·

1

Is Arendelle a real place?

While Arendelle is a fictional place, its name comes from an actual town in Norway called Arendal. Elsa and Anna's imaginary kingdom does not exactly resemble this town, though.

Much of Arendelle's architecture was influenced by other Norwegian locations. The styles of buildings and their natural surroundings helped to form the kingdom's appearance.

princess	공주
secret	비밀
power	힘

ballroom	무도회장
sled	썰매를 타다

troll	(전설 속) 트롤
worry	걱정하다
fear	두려워하다

castle　성

spill　쏟아져 나오다

fill	가득 채우다	Elsa filled an empty room with snow.
empty	비어 있는	

lose control	통제력을 잃다	Elsa lost control while she was playing with her sister.

accidentally	우연히	Elsa accidentally hit Anna with a frozen blast.
blast	강한 바람	

badly	심하게	Anna was badly injured.

ancient	고대의	An ancient and wise troll helped the royal family.
wise	현명한	

get better	좋아지다	Anna got better with the help of the trolls.

gift	재능	The King and Queen wanted to keep Elsa's gift a secret.

surround	둘러싸다	The castle was surrounded by walls.

Vocabulary

crown	왕관을 씌우다
ceremony	의식
coronation	대관식

handsome 잘생긴

shoot 발사되다
(과거형 shot)

stare 빤히 쳐다보다

panic 어쩔 줄 모르다
(과거형 panicked)

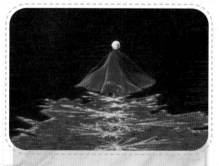

flee 달아나다 (과거형 fled)

lost	실종된	The King and Queen were **lost** at sea.
attend	참석하다	Hundreds of people **attend**ed the party.
southern isle	남쪽에 위치한 섬	Anna danced with Prince Hans from the **Southern Isle**s.
flutter	(심장 등이) 두근거리다	Anna's heart **fluttered** when she was with Hans.
have in common	~라는 공통점이 있다	Seemingly, Anna **had** a lot **in common** with Hans.
blessing engagement	승인, 허락 약혼	Anna and Hans asked Elsa to give her **blessing** to their engagement.
shut out	~을 제외시키다	Anna did not know why her sister **shut** her **out**.
afraid	두려워하는	Anna did not understand what her sister was **afraid** of.

Vocabulary Quiz

1 Find hidden words in the puzzle below. Then write down the correct meaning accordingly.

M	L	E	X	Y	B	T	R	G	U	V	C
C	D	N	W	B	L	I	U	F	L	E	E
O	X	G	B	R	A	C	K	S	M	A	N
R	S	A	C	L	S	V	I	Y	U	R	G
O	W	G	F	Z	T	V	O	P	E	S	K
N	C	E	R	E	M	O	N	Y	Q	T	L
A	G	M	B	N	D	D	R	Q	S	A	W
T	P	E	P	G	D	P	X	I	D	R	N
I	O	N	Q	Z	F	L	U	T	T	E	R
O	Z	T	H	H	T	X	H	J	K	Y	Z
N	R	U	A	F	R	A	I	D	H	F	V
N	J	A	T	T	E	N	D	X	G	N	D

flee	달아나다	stare		coronation	
blast		flutter		ceremony	
afraid		engagement		attend	

2 **Fill in the missing letters for each word. Then complete the answer to the quiz.**

① <u>h</u>andsome 잘생긴

② __ccidentally 우연히

③ crow__ 왕관을 씌우다

④ __ift 재능

⑤ w__rry 걱정하다

⑥ s__rround 둘러싸다

⑦ __roll (전설 속) 트롤

⑧ fe__r 두려워하다

⑨ a__cient 고대의

⑩ empt__ 비어 있는

⑪ have in com__ __n ~라는 공통점이 있다 *two letters

⑫ p__incess 공주

⑬ s__cret 비밀

QUIZ

What happened after the terrible accident between sisters?

ANSWER

Elsa and Anna did not

<u>h</u>___ ___ _____.

1 Look at the pictures and the description below. Then number them in the correct order to match the story.

Anna knew Elsa's secret: she had a magic power.

1

Elsa lost control of her power at the ceremony.

Anna fell in love with Prince Hans at first sight.

Anna did not know why Elsa was not around.

2 Choose the best answer for each question.

1 Why did Elsa's parents close the castle?

a) They did not want Elsa to hurt Anna again.

b) They were angry at Elsa for having the power.

c) They were worried about how people would react to Elsa's power.

2 Why did Anna feel lonely?

a) Because Elsa did not play with Anna anymore

b) Because her parents left Anna alone in the castle

c) Because Elsa was too busy playing with other friends

3 How did people find out about Elsa's power?

a) Elsa shot ice to save Anna.

b) Anna told everyone about it at the party.

c) Elsa accidentally released a blast of ice at the party.

3 Read each sentence and decide whether it is true or false.

1 When Elsa and Anna were young, they were very close.	true	false
2 Elsa's parents were proud of Elsa's power.	true	false
3 Anna did not like meeting the people of Arendelle.	true	false
4 Anna became the queen of Arendelle.	true	false
5 Anna danced with Prince Hans and fell in love with him.	true	false

· Part ·

2

Outfits for characters

Traditional Norwegian folk-dancing clothing led to the creation of Anna's and Elsa's dresses. Such clothing may not be commonly seen in everyday life now.

However, these unique costumes can be found on display at a folk museum in Oslo. In addition, Kristoff's clothing was inspired by the clothing of an indigenous group of people.

Vocabulary

kingdom 왕국

race 쏜살같이 가다
ride (말 등을) 타다 (과거형 rode)

harvester 수확을 돕는 일꾼

reindeer [동물] 순록

climb 오르다

| **horrible** | 끔찍한 | Anna felt **horrible** for what had happened to Arendelle. |

create	창조하다	
terrible	극심한	Elsa had **created** a **terrible** winter **storm** in Arendelle.
storm	폭풍	

| **in charge of** | ~을 책임진 | Hans was **in charge of** looking after the people of Arendelle. |

| **fierce** | 맹렬한 | Anna went through the **fierce** wind. |

| **set off** | 출발하다 | Anna **set off** to **look for** Elsa with her new friends, Kristoff and Sven. |
| **look for** | ~을 찾다 | |

| **discover** | 발견하다 | Anna and Kristoff **discovered** a beautiful winter forest. |

| **enchanted** | 마법에 걸린 | Anna thought that she had met the **enchanted** snowman before. |

| **get to the point** | 요점을 말하다 | Kristoff **got to the point** and told Olaf the truth. |

wonderland 아주 멋진 곳

crowd 사람들

soldier 군인

giant 거대한
palace 궁전

impressed 감명을 받은

be eager to	~하고 싶어 하다	Olaf **was eager to** take Anna to Elsa.
meanwhile	그동안에	**Meanwhile**, Hans helped the people of Arendelle.
hard at work	열심히 일하는	Hans was **hard at work** taking care of the kingdom.
without	~ 없이	Anna's horse came back to the castle **without** Anna.
volunteer	지원자	Hans needed **volunteers** to go with him.
set out in search of	출발하다 ~을 찾아서	Hans **set out** in search of Anna and Elsa.
lead	안내하다 (과거형 led)	Olaf **led** Anna and Kristoff to Elsa.
unfreeze	녹이다	Anna was sure that Elsa could **unfreeze** Arendelle.
worse	더 악화된	Elsa worried that she would make everything **worse**.
be better off	~하는 것이 더 낫다	Elsa thought that Anna **was better off** without her.

Vocabulary Quiz

1 Use the clues below to fill in the crossword puzzle.

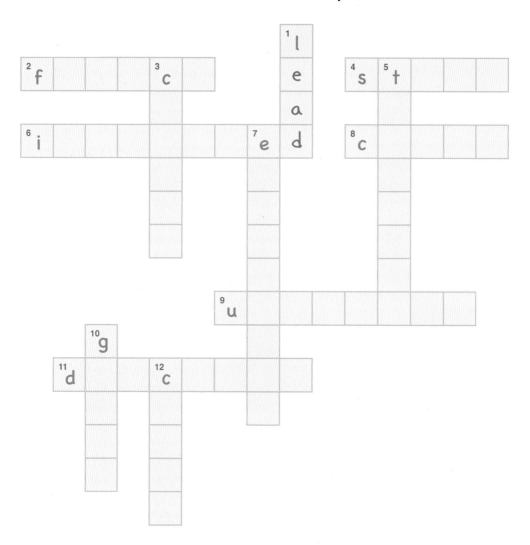

2 Fill in the missing letters for each word. Then complete the answer to the quiz.

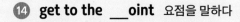

1 hor__ible 끔찍한   **2** p__lace 궁전

3 i__ ch__rge o__ ~을 책임진 *three letters   **4** wi__hout ~ 없이

5 s__t out 출발하다   **6** __ace 쏜살같이 가다

7 me__nwhile 그동안에   **8** wor__e 더 악화된

9 __ingdom 왕국   **10** be __ager to ~하고 싶어 하다

11 ri__e (말 등을) 타다   **12** __ard at work 열심히 일하는

13 wond__r__and 아주 멋진 곳 *two letters

14 get to the __oint 요점을 말하다

Comprehension Quiz

1 Choose the sentence which best describes the picture to match the story.

Ⓐ Anna warned Kristoff to leave the forest.

Ⓑ Anna asked Kristoff and Sven to help her find Elsa.

Ⓒ Anna helped Kristoff and Sven make a snowman.

Ⓐ Hans returned to the castle with Elsa's horse.

Ⓑ Hans told people that he would go back to the Southern Isles.

Ⓒ Hans gathered some people to search for Anna.

2 Choose the best answer for each question.

1 Why did Anna look for Elsa?

a) To be the queen of Arendelle

b) To learn how to get the magical power

c) To have Elsa bring summer back to Arendelle

2 Who did Anna meet after her horse left her in the forest?

a) Elsa and Olaf

b) Kristoff and Sven

c) Prince Hans and his soldiers

3 Why was Elsa afraid of going back to Arendelle?

a) Because she loved living alone in the ice palace

b) Because she would make the storm worse

c) Because she thought that people would attack her

3 Read each sentence and decide whether it is true or false.

❶ Anna set out to the forest to bring back Elsa.	true	false
❷ Olaf did not know where Elsa was.	true	false
❸ Hans fled to the Southern Isles.	true	false
❹ Kristoff was amazed at the ice palace built by Elsa.	true	false
❺ Elsa already knew how to unfreeze Arendelle.	true	false

🔊 Listen and read the characters' words.

Listen to the "Listen & Read Along" audio file and repeat after each sentence, focusing on your pause (**/**), stress (**bold**), and linking (⌒).

Can I say **some**thing **cra**zy?

You **can't** marry a man you just **met**.

I'll bring her back, / and I'll make this **right**.

· Part ·

3

How did trolls become a part of the story?

Some Norwegian tales include trolls with magical powers. The folk stories are learned from a young age. This makes trolls well-known creatures that may even seem real to kids.

One city in Norway actually has a "troll forest," where visitors can walk around and feel a magical atmosphere.

Vocabulary

argue 언쟁을 하다

burst 터지다, 파열하다
(과거형 burst)

huge 거대한

hurry 서두르다
toward ~을 향해

arrive 도착하다

try	~을 해 보다	Anna **tried** to talk with her sister.
convince	설득하다	Anna wanted to **convince** Elsa to come home.
scared	무서워하는	Elsa was **scared** that she would **hurt** people.
hurt	다치게 하다	
wave	파동	An icy **wave** of magic **struck** Anna in the **chest**.
strike	치다, 때리다 (과거형 struck)	
chest	가슴	
chase out of	~에서 쫓아내다	A huge snowman **chased** Anna and Kristoff **out of** the palace.
cliff	절벽	Anna and Kristoff stood on a tall **cliff**.
land	(땅에) 떨어지다	Kristoff thought that falling from the cliff would be like **landing** on a **pillow**.
pillow	베개	
leap	뛰어오르다	Anna and Kristoff **leaped** from the **edge** of the cliff.
edge	끝, 가장자리	

Vocabulary

attack   공격하다

defend   방어하다

trap   (위험한 장소에) 가두다
spike   (못같이) 뾰족한 것

dungeon   지하 감옥

fluffy	푹신해 보이는	Anna and Kristoff fell on the fluffy snow.
reverse	뒤바꾸다	The magic had to be reversed to save Anna.
freeze	얼어붙다 (과거분사형 frozen)	Anna would be frozen solid without help.
thaw	녹이다	There was a way to thaw a frozen heart.
shiver	(몸을) 떨다	Anna shivered as she felt herself getting weak.
care for	~를 좋아하다	Kristoff realized that he cared for Anna.
cry out	외치다	Hans cried out to Elsa not to be a monster.
monster	괴물	
pause	잠시 멈추다	Elsa paused as she had a doubt.
doubt	의심	
knock out	의식을 잃게 하다	Elsa was knocked out by the soldiers.

Vocabulary Quiz

1 Find hidden words in the puzzle below. Then write down the correct
meaning accordingly.

L	H	D	E	V	A	N	J	G	U	K	P
C	U	Z	W	A	R	G	U	E	F	S	M
M	R	I	V	K	E	J	W	C	N	D	U
I	T	U	B	C	V	Y	V	R	N	X	J
V	H	M	I	M	E	D	E	F	E	N	D
X	J	C	H	U	R	R	Y	B	C	B	Z
C	G	Y	C	P	S	C	X	X	R	D	F
H	B	A	H	D	E	G	Q	M	Q	O	Y
T	K	Q	T	G	N	J	B	A	K	U	J
R	E	E	D	G	E	U	A	I	T	B	Y
A	S	E	C	I	T	Q	Q	J	V	T	W
P	B	S	T	R	I	K	E	R	I	S	U

hurt		strike		reverse	
doubt		argue		defend	
hurry		edge		trap	

34 · Frozen

2 Fill in the missing letters for each word. Then complete the answer to the quiz.

① __pike 뾰족한 것

② __ry ~을 해 보다

③ a__rive 도착하다

④ b__rst 터지다

⑤ __hase out of ~에서 쫓아내다

⑥ knoc__ out 의식을 잃게 하다

⑦ sh__ver (몸을) 떨다

⑧ s__ared 무서워하는

⑨ fluff__ 푹신해 보이는

⑩ tha__ 녹이다

⑪ c__re for ~를 좋아하다

⑫ con__ince 설득하다

⑬ fre__ze 얼어붙다

QUIZ

What happened when Anna argued with Elsa about going back to Arendelle?

ANSWER

Elsa _ _ _ _ _ _ _ Anna with an

_ _ _ _ _ _ _ _ of magic.

Comprehension Quiz

1 Look at the pictures and the description below. Then number them in the correct order to match the story.

 Kristoff brought Anna back to Arendelle to save her.

 Elsa created a huge snowman to send Anna and Kristoff away.

 The soldiers locked Elsa in the dungeon.

 Trolls told Kristoff and Anna how to break the spell.

2 Choose the best answer for each question.

1 Why did Elsa make a huge snowman?

a) Because Anna refused to leave Elsa

b) Because Elsa wanted to show her power

c) Because Olaf asked Elsa to make a friend for him

2 Which did NOT happen to Anna and Kristoff when they left the palace?

a) They went to see the trolls to get help.

b) They were chased by a huge snowman.

c) They got separated when they fell from the cliff.

3 What happened to Elsa after Anna and Kristoff had left?

a) She created a lot of giant snowmen.

b) She had to defend herself from the soldiers.

c) She lost all of her power and came back to Arendelle.

3 Read each sentence and decide whether it is true or false.

1 Elsa asked Anna to live with her in the ice palace.	true	false
2 Elsa was afraid that she would hurt more people.	true	false
3 Elsa's power hit Anna in the legs.	true	false
4 Kristoff and Anna became friends with a huge snowman.	true	false
5 Hans and his soldiers went to the ice palace to save Elsa.	true	false

· Part ·
4

Fun Fact

A particular church was significant for two characters.

When Elsa is officially crowned queen, her ceremony is held in a chapel.

A Norwegian church inspired the look of this location. And the church happens to be named St. Olaf's Church. This ended up becoming the name of Elsa's snowman, Olaf.

warm 따뜻하게 하다

weak 약한

evil 사악한
plan 계획

glance 흘깃 보다

| **refuse** | 거절하다 | Hans **refused** to save Anna. |

| **realize** **pretend** | 깨닫다 ~인 척하다 | Anna **realized** that Hans had **pretend**ed to love her. |

| **take over** | 장악하다 | Hans's plan was to **take over** Arendelle. |

| **get rid of** | 제거하다 | Hans needed to **get rid of** both sisters. |

| **strength** | 힘 | Her **strength** fading, Anna went outside. |

| **escape** | 탈출하다 | Elsa managed to **escape** from the dungeon. |

| **protect** **fail** | 보호하다 실패하다 | All Elsa ever wanted was to **protect** her sister, but she **fail**ed. |

| **fault** | 잘못, 책임 | Elsa believed that it was her **fault** for not protecting Anna. |

| **nearby** | 인근에 | Kristoff was **nearby**, hoping Anna was okay. |

Vocabulary

struggle   힘겹게 움직이다

collapse   쓰러지다

solid   단단한

clutch   (꽉) 움켜잡다
reach   ~에 닿다

| clang | 쨍그랑 하는 소리 | Anna heard the **clang** of Hans's **sword**. |
| **sword** | 검, 칼 | |

| **danger** | 위험 | Anna found out that Elsa was in **danger**. |

| **instead of** | ~ 대신에 | Anna tried to save Elsa, **instead of** herself. |

| **swing** | 휘두르다
(과거형 swung) | Hans **swung** his sword at Elsa. |

| **shatter** | 산산이 부서지다 | The sword **shattered** against Anna's body. |
| **against** | ~에 부딪쳐 | |

| **keep from** | ~하는 것을 막다 | Elsa used her magic to **keep** Olaf **from** **melt**ing. |
| **melt** | 녹다 | |

| **surprise** | 놀라운 일 | Elsa had a **surprise** for her sister. |

| **be supposed to** | ~하기로
되어 있다 | Everything was peaceful, as it **was supposed to** be. |

Vocabulary Quiz

1 Use the clues below to fill in the crossword puzzle.

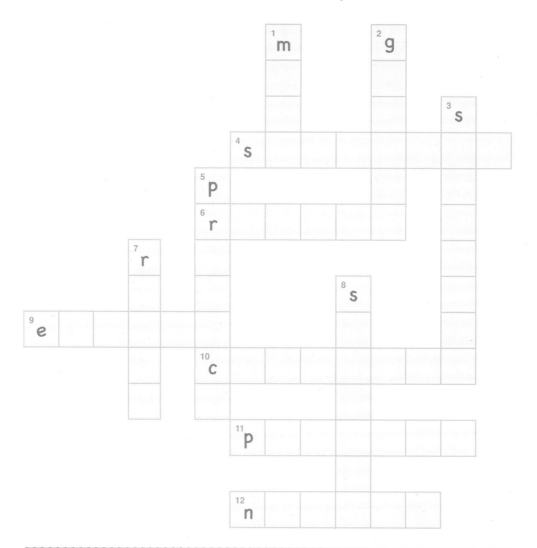

2 **Fill in the missing letters for each word. Then complete the answer to the quiz.**

1 clu__c__ (꽉) 움켜잡다 *two letters

2 __gainst ~에 부딪쳐

3 s__ord 검, 칼

4 be __upposed to ~하기로 되어 있다

5 f__ult 잘못, 책임

6 e__il 사악한

7 inst__ad of ~ 대신에

8 __eep from ~하는 것을 막다

9 fa__l 실패하다

10 cla__ __ 쨍그랑 하는 소리 *two letters

11 __anger 위험

12 s__lid 단단한

13 war__ 따뜻하게 하다

QUIZ

What happened when Elsa touched Anna's frozen body?

ANSWER

Anna started to _____ and Elsa and Anna were

able to _____ the _____ .

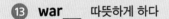

Comprehension **Quiz**

1 Choose the sentence which best describes the picture to match the story.

A Hans had pretended to care for Anna.

B Anna and Hans really missed each other.

C Anna realized that she did not love Hans.

A Elsa searched for Anna in the middle of storm.

B Elsa stopped Anna from going to Kristoff.

C Anna's love for Elsa saved her own life.

2 Choose the best answer for each question.

1 What was Hans's plan?

a) To marry Elsa

b) To help the people of Arendelle

c) To take over Arendelle

2 How did Elsa survive Hans's attack?

a) Elsa gave up and let him be the king of Arendelle.

b) Anna stepped in and protected Elsa from him.

c) Elsa ducked down to avoid his sword.

3 Which did NOT happen after Anna and Elsa saved the kingdom?

a) Summer returned to Arendelle.

b) Elsa made a little snow cloud for Olaf.

c) The castle gates were closed again.

3 Read each sentence and decide whether it is true or false.

1 Hans's kiss made Anna get better.	true	false
2 Too discouraged, Kristoff did not come back to the castle.	true	false
3 Hans helped Elsa escape from the dungeon.	true	false
4 Anna jumped in front of Elsa to save her.	true	false
5 Elsa promised not to close the castle gates again.	true	false

Listen and Read Along

🔊 **Listen and read the characters' words.**

Listen to the "Listen & Read Along" audio file and repeat after each sentence, focusing on your pause (**/**), stress (**bold**), and linking (⌢).

No. / I'm **not** leaving with**out** you, Elsa.

What if we **fall**?

It will be like **land**ing on a **pill**ow / hopefully.

Story Map

⭐ Follow the story line and put the stickers on their correct places!

START

1

Princess Elsa had a magical power to make ice and snow.

4

As she was looking for Elsa, Anna met Kristoff, Sven, and Olaf.

5

Elsa argued with Anna and struck her with the magical power.

FINISH

8

The kingdom was saved by Anna's true love for Elsa.

2 After Elsa hurt Anna, their parents locked up the castle to hide Elsa.

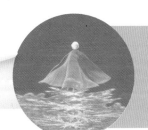

3 At the coronation, Elsa's power was revealed and she fled out of fear.

6 Anna and Kristoff found out that an act of true love could end the curse.

7 Anna learned Hans's evil plan to take over Arendelle.

Character Chart

✏ **Choose your favorite character and describe them using the words from the personality bank.**

Personality Bank

generous 관대한	**sweet** 상냥한	**optimistic** 낙관적인
elegant 우아한	**ambitious** 야심 있는	**perky** 활발한
welcoming 따뜻한	**playful** 장난기 많은	**cruel** 잔인한
loyal 충성스러운	**clever** 똑똑한	**innocent** 순수한

Stick Here!

My favorite character is

_____ .

I think _____ is

_____ ,

_____ , and

_____ .

* There is an example answer for you to refer to on page 63.

Disney FROZEN

Read Along

· Translation ·

Translation

p.2

❄ 아렌델의 엘사 공주와 안나 공주가 어린 소녀였을 때, 그들은 가장 친한 친구사이였습니다. 안나는 엘사의 비밀을 아는 유일한 사람들 중 한 사람이었습니다: 엘사는 자신의 두 손만으로 눈과 얼음을 만드는 힘을 지니고 있었어요!

어느 밤, 엘사는 빈 연회장을 눈으로 가득 채웠습니다. 자매는 눈사람을 만들고, 썰매를 타고, 그리고 아이스 스케이트도 타면서, 함께 놀았습니다.

p.3

❄ 하지만 그들이 놀던 중, 엘사가 통제력을 잃었습니다. 그녀는 실수로 한 줄기의 얼음 마법으로 안나를 맞추고 말았어요! 안나가 심하게 다치자, 그녀의 부모님은 도움을 청하러 고대 마운틴 트롤들에게 갔습니다. 그곳에서, 현명하고 나이 든 트롤이 안나를 살릴 수 있으며—심장이 아니라, 머리에 맞았기에 그녀가 운이 좋았다고 그들에게 말했습니다.

p.4

❄ 비록 안나는 괜찮아졌지만, 그녀의 부모님은 사람들이 엘사의 힘을 두려워할까 봐 걱정했습니다. 그녀의 능력을 비밀로 하기 위해, 그들은 성을 벽으로 둘러쌌고 아무도 안으로 들이지 않았습니다.

하지만 엘사가 강한 감정을 느낄 때마다, 마법은 여전히 밖으로 쏟아져 나왔습니다. 엘사는 다시는 자신의 여동생을 다치게 하고 싶지 않아서, 그녀는 절대로 안나와 놀지 않았습니다. 이는 안나를 매우 외롭게 했죠.

심지어 바다에서 그들의 부모님이 폭풍에 실종된 후에도, 자매는 함께 시간을 보내지 않았습니다.

❄ 몇 년이 흐른 뒤, 엘사가 아렌델의 여왕이 될 때가 되었습니다. 오직 그날만을 위해, 성문이 열렸습니다! 수백 명의 사람들이 대관식에 참석했습니다. 엘사는 자신의 감정을—그리고 자신의 힘을 숨기려고 열심히 노력했습니다!

안나는 그 모든 새로운 사람들을 만나는 것을 정말 좋아했습니다. "난 언제나 이랬으면 좋겠어."

"나도, 그래."

❄ 대관식 파티에서, 안나는 남부 제도에서 온 잘생긴 한스 왕자와 춤을 추었습니다. 그는 그녀의 마음을 두근거리게 했지요. 그들은 모든 일에 공통점을 지니고 있는 것처럼 보였습니다.

❄ 성문이 단 하루만 열렸기 때문에, 한스와 안나는 이 순간이 그들이 함께할 수 있는 유일한 기회라는 것을 알았습니다. "제가 이상한 말을 해도 될까요? 저와 결혼해 주시겠어요?"

"좋아요!"

❄ 안나와 한스는 엘사에게 그녀의 허락을 구했습니다. 하지만 엘사는 그들의 약혼이 좋은 생각이 아니라고 생각했습니다. "너는 방금 만난 남자와 결혼할 수 없어. 허락할 수 없다는 게 바로 내 대답이야."

안나는 그 말을 믿을 수 없었습니다. "언니는 왜 나를 밀어내는 거야? 언니는 무엇을 그렇게 두려워하는 거야?"

p.9

❄ 엘사는 통제력을 잃기 시작했습니다. "그만해!" 그녀가 외치자, 얼음이 그녀의 두 손에서 발사되었습니다. 모든 사람이 놀라서 엘사를 바라보았어요. 이제 아렌델의 모든 사람이 엘사의 비밀을 알게 되었습니다! 엘사는 어쩔 줄 몰라 했고 산으로 도망쳐 버렸습니다.

p.10

❄ 안나는 정말 마음이 좋지 않았어요! 엘사의 통제에서 벗어난 힘이 엄청난 겨울 폭풍을 일으켰습니다—그것도 바로 한여름에 말이에요! "제가 언니를 데려올게요, 그리고 이 일을 바로 잡겠어요." 그녀는 한스에게 왕국을 맡겼고, 자신의 말에 올라 엘사를 쫓아 급히 달려갔습니다.

　하지만 안나가 세찬 바람을 뚫고 달려갔을 때, 그녀의 말은 그녀를 눈 속에 던지고 다시 아렌델로 달려가 버렸습니다.

p.11

❄ 다행히도, 안나는 크리스토프라는 이름의 얼음 채취꾼과 그의 순록 친구인 스벤을 만났습니다. 그녀는 그들에게 도움을 청했어요. "나는 이 겨울을 끝낼 방법을 알고 있어요."

　함께, 그들은 엘사를 찾아 나섰습니다.

p.12

❄ 그들이 산에 올랐을 때, 안나와 크리스토프는 동화에 나올 법한 아름다운 겨울 나라를 발견했습니다. 그곳에서, 그들은 올라프라는 이름의 마법에 걸린 눈사람을 만났어요. 안나는 그가 친숙하게 보인다고 생각했습니다. "올라프, 엘사가 너를 만들었니?"

　올라프가 미소 지었습니다. "응. 왜?"

p.13

❄ "넌 그녀가 어디에 있는지 아니?"

　"응. 왜?"

　크리스토프는 요점을 바로 말했습니다. "우리는 여름을 되돌리기 위해 엘사가 필요해."

　올라프는 몹시 그들을 돕고 싶었습니다. "따라와!"

p.14

❄ 그동안에, 한스는 열심히 일하며 아렌델의 국민들을 돕고 있었습니다. 하지만 안나의 말이 그녀 없이 성으로 돌아오자, 한스는 자신이 가만히 있을 수 없다는 것을 알았습니다.

"안나 공주에게 문제가 생겼어요." 한스는 사람들을 향해 돌아섰습니다. "그녀를 찾기 위해 저와 함께 갈 지원자들이 필요합니다!" 곧, 한스와 몇 명의 군인들이 안나—그리고 엘사를—찾기 위해 출발했습니다.

p.15

❄ 다시 산 위에서는, 올라프가 안나와 크리스토프를 엘사가 자신의 힘으로 만들어 낸 거대한 얼음 궁전으로 데려갔습니다.

심지어 크리스토프도 경이로워했습니다. "이게 진짜 얼음이지."

p.16

❄ 안에서, 안나는 엘사에게 아렌델에 닥친 엄청난 폭풍에 대해 말했습니다. "괜찮아. 언니는 그냥 그것을 녹이면 돼."

엘사는 걱정스러워 보였습니다. "나는 방법을 몰라."

"좋지 않은 소식이네."

p.17

❄ 엘사는 만약에 그녀가 돌아간다면, 자신이 폭풍을 악화시킬까 봐 겁이 났습니다. 아렌델에—그리고 안나에게—그녀가 없는 편이 더 나을 것 같았습니다. "내가 어떻게 해야 하지?"

p.18

❄ 안나는 엘사에게 집으로 돌아가자고 설득하기 위해 노력하고 또 노력했습니다. 하지만 엘사는 자신이 더 많은 사람들을 다치게 할까 봐 몹시 두려웠습니다. 엘사가 자신의 여동생과 말다툼을 하는 동안, 얼음같이 찬 마법 파장이 그녀의 몸에서 뿜어져 나왔고—안나의 가슴을 맞췄습니다!

"안나!"

p.19

❄ 안나는 일어섰고 엘사를 바라보았습니다. "아니야. 엘사, 나는 언니 없이는 떠나지 않을 거야."

"아니, 너는 나 없이 떠나게 될 거야." 엘사는 자신이 무엇을 해야만 하는지 알았습니다.

p.20

❄ 엘사는 자신의 마법을 사용해서 거대한 눈사람을 만들어 냈습니다. 그는 궁전 밖으로 그리고 높은 절벽으로 친구들을 쫓아냈습니다.

크리스토프는 그들이 내려가는 것을 도와줄 밧줄을 꺼냈습니다.

"우리가 떨어지면 어떡해요?"

"저 아래에는 20피트(약 6.1미터)의 새로 쌓인 고운 눈이 있어요. 그건 베개 위로 떨어지는 것과 같을 거예요... 바라건대 말이죠."

그들은 가장자리 너머로 뛰었고, 아래에 쌓인 폭신폭신한 눈 위로 안전하게 떨어졌습니다. 그들은 눈사람에서 도망쳤지만, 안나에게는 걱정해야 할 다른 일이 있었습니다...

p.22

❄ 안나의 머리카락이 눈처럼 하얗게 변하고 있었거든요!

"그녀가 당신을 공격했기 때문이죠, 그렇지 않나요?" 크리스토프는 트롤들이 도와줄 수 있기를 바라며, 그들에게 안나를 데려갔습니다. 한 트롤이 그들에게 엘사의 얼음 마법이 안나의 심장을 맞췄다고 말했습니다. 만약에 마법을 되돌리지 못한다면, 안나는 곧 단단히 얼어붙게 될 것이었습니다. 오직 진정한 사랑의 행동만이 얼어붙은 심장을 녹일 수 있었습니다.

p.23

❄ 안나는 자신이 한스를 사랑한다는 것을 알았습니다—어쩌면 그의 키스가 통할지도 몰랐습니다! 친구들이 서둘러서 아렌델로 향하는 동안, 안나는 몸을 떨기 시작했습니다. 크리스토프는 특히 그녀에 대해 걱정했습니다. 그는 안나에게 마음이 가기 시작하고 있었습니다.

---

p.24

❄ 바로 그때, 한스와 그의 군인들은 얼음 궁전에 이르렀고 엘사를 공격했습니다. 그녀가 자신을 방어하면서, 엘사는 그녀를 공격하는 사람들 가운데 한 사람을 뾰족하게 솟아오른 얼음 뒤에 가두었습니다.

한스가 그녀에게 외쳤습니다. "엘사 여왕님! 사람들이 두려워하는 괴물이 되지 마세요!"

---

p.25

❄ 엘사는 멈칫했고, 그녀가 의심하는 순간에, 그녀는 의식을 잃고 쓰러졌습니다. 공격자들은 그녀를 아렌델로 데려갔고 그녀를 지하 감옥 안에 던져 넣었습니다.

---

p.26

❄ 안나가 아렌델에 도착했을 때, 그녀는 크리스토프와 올라프에게 작별 인사를 했습니다. 그러고 나서, 그녀는 한스를 만나기 위해 급히 달려갔습니다.

그들이 홀로 남게 되자마자, 안나는 한스에게 키스로 자신을 구해달라고 부탁했습니다. 하지만 한스는 거절했습니다! 안나는 그가 그녀를 사랑하는 척했을 뿐이라는 것을 깨달았습니다.

그는 안나와 엘사를 없애서 아렌델을 차지하길 원했습니다! "이제 남은 일은 엘사를 죽이고 여름을 되돌리는 것뿐이야."

p.27

❄ 한스는 안나를 홀로 덜덜 떨도록 내버려 두고 떠났습니다. 다행스럽게도, 올라프가 그녀를 찾아냈고 불가에서 그녀가 몸을 녹이는 것을 도와주었습니다. 하지만 안나는 여전히 점점 더 약해져만 갔습니다.

안나가 그에게 한스의 사악한 계획에 대해 말했을 때, 올라프는 창밖을 힐끗 보았고 성을 향해 크리스토프가 빠르게 달려오는 것을 보았습니다. 그는 크리스토프가 안나를 사랑한다는 것을 깨달았습니다. "너를 위한 진정한 사랑의 행동이 바로 저기에 있어!" 안나가 키스해야 할 사람은 바로 크리스토프였어요! 자신의 마지막 힘을 다해서, 안나는 밖으로 힘겹게 나갔습니다.

p.28

❄ 한편, 엘사는 지하 감옥에서 탈출했지만, 한스가 그녀를 바짝 따라왔습니다. "엘사, 당신은 이 일에서 도망칠 수 없어요." 한스는 엘사에게 안나의 심장에 꽂힌 그녀의 마법 공격에 대해 말해 주었습니다. "전 그녀를 구하려고 했지만, 너무 늦고 말았어요."

p.29

❄ 엘사는 눈 속에서 쓰러졌고 자신의 두 눈을 감았습니다. 그녀가 자신의 여동생을 보호하기 위해 해 왔던 모든 일이 실패했습니다. 그리고 그것은 모두 그녀의 잘못이었습니다.

가까이에서, 안나가 크리스토프를 향해 서둘러서 가고 있을 때 그녀는 한스의 검에서 나는 쨍그랑 하는 소리를 듣게 되었습니다. 그녀는 돌아서서 자신의 언니를 보았습니다—엘사가 위험에 처해 있었습니다!

p.30

❄ 자신을 구하려고 크리스토프에게 달려가는 대신에, 안나는 자기 언니 앞으로 뛰어들었습니다. "안 돼!"

한스가 그의 검을 휘두르자, 그것은 안나의 얼어붙은 몸에 맞아 산산조각이 났습니다. 그녀의 몸은 단단한 얼음으로 변해 버렸습니다.

p.31

❄ 엘사는 자신의 여동생을 꼭 끌어안았습니다. "오, 안나. 안 돼. 제발, 안 돼!" 갑자기, 안나의 몸이 녹기 시작했습니다! 그녀의 두 팔이, 다시 따뜻해져서, 엘사를 감쌌고, 두 자매는 포옹했습니다.

올라프가 그들을 바라보았을 때, 그는 현명하고 나이 든 트롤이 했던 말을 기억했습니다: "진정한 사랑의 행동이 얼어붙은 심장을 녹일 수 있어." 엘사에 대한 안나의 사랑이 그 두 사람 모두를—그리고 왕국을 구해 낸 것이었습니다.

p.32

❄ 곧 두 자매는 다시 가장 친한 친구 사이가 되었고, 다시 아렌델에는 여름이 돌아왔습니다. 엘사는 심지어 올라프에게 그가 녹는 것을 막아 줄 작은 눈구름도 만들어 주었습니다.

어느 날, 엘사는 안나를 위해 깜짝 선물을 준비했습니다—바로 활짝 열린 성문이었습니다! "우리는 절대로 그것들을 다시 닫지 않을 거야."

자매는 서로를 향해 미소 지었습니다. 이제 모든 것이 원래 그랬어야 했던 모습으로 돌아오게 되었습니다.

Vocabulary Quiz

1

M	L	E	X	Y	B	T	R	G	U	V	C
C	D	N	W	B	L	I	U	F	L	E	E
O	X	G	B	R	A	C	K	S	M	A	N
R	S	A	C	L	S	V	I	Y	U	R	G
O	W	G	F	Z	T	V	O	P	E	S	K
N	C	E	R	E	M	O	N	Y	Q	T	L
A	G	M	B	N	D	D	R	Q	S	A	W
T	P	E	P	G	D	P	X	I	D	R	N
I	O	N	Q	Z	F	L	U	T	T	E	R
O	Z	T	H	H	T	X	H	J	K	Y	Z
N	R	U	A	F	R	A	I	D	H	F	V
N	J	A	T	T	E	N	D	X	G	N	D

flee 달아나다 / **stare** 빤히 쳐다보다 /
coronation 대관식 / **blast** 강한 바람 /
flutter (심장 등이) 두근거리다 /
ceremony 의식 / **afraid** 두려워하는 /
engagement 약혼 / **attend** 참석하다

2   1 handsome   2 accidentally
    3 crown   4 gift   5 worry
    6 surround   7 troll   8 fear
    9 ancient   10 empty
    11 have in common
    12 princess   13 secret

| ANSWER
Elsa and Anna did not hang out
anymore.

Comprehension Quiz

1   1 - 4 - 3 - 2

2   1 c   2 a   3 c

3   1 true   2 false   3 false
    4 false   5 true

Vocabulary Quiz

1

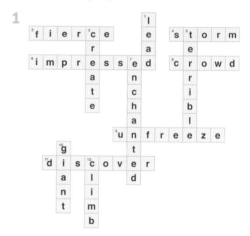

2   1 horrible   2 palace   3 in charge of
    4 without   5 set out   6 race
    7 meanwhile   8 worse   9 kingdom
    10 be eager to   11 ride
    12 hard at work   13 wonderland
    14 get to the point

| ANSWER
Anna ran after Elsa and asked
Kristoff and Sven for help.

Comprehension Quiz

1   1 b   2 c

2   1 c   2 b   3 b

3   1 true   2 false   3 false
    4 true   5 false

Vocabulary Quiz

1

L	H	D	E	V	A	N	J	G	U	K	P
C	U	Z	W	A	R	G	U	E	F	S	M
M	R	I	V	K	E	J	W	C	N	D	U
I	T	U	B	C	V	Y	V	R	N	X	J
V	H	M	I	M	E	D	E	F	E	N	D
X	J	C	H	U	R	R	Y	B	C	B	Z
C	G	Y	C	P	S	C	X	X	R	D	F
H	B	A	H	D	E	G	Q	M	Q	O	Y
T	K	Q	T	G	N	J	B	A	K	U	J
R	E	E	D	G	E	U	A	I	T	B	Y
A	S	E	C	I	T	Q	Q	J	V	T	W
P	B	S	T	R	I	K	E	R	I	S	U

hurt 다치게 하다 / **strike** 치다, 때리다 /
reverse 뒤바꾸다 / **doubt** 의심 /
argue 언쟁을 하다 / **defend** 방어하다 /
hurry 서두르다 / **edge** 끝, 가장자리 /
trap (위험한 장소에) 가두다

2 1 spike   2 try   3 arrive   4 burst
5 chase out of   6 knock out
7 shiver   8 scared   9 fluffy
10 thaw   11 care for
12 convince   13 freeze

| ANSWER
Elsa struck Anna with an icy wave
of magic.

Comprehension Quiz

1 3 - 1 - 4 - 2
2 1 a   2 c   3 b
3 1 false   2 true   3 false
4 false   5 false

Vocabulary Quiz

1

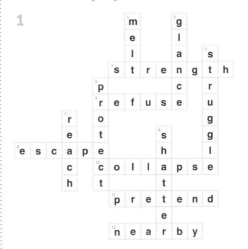

2 1 clutch   2 against   3 sword
4 be supposed to   5 fault   6 evil
7 instead of   8 keep from   9 fail
10 clang   11 danger   12 solid
13 warm

| ANSWER
Anna started to thaw and Elsa
and Anna were able to save the
kingdom.

Comprehension Quiz

1 1 a   2 c
2 1 c   2 b   3 c
3 1 false   2 false   3 false
4 true   5 true

Character Chart   p.48

| EXAMPLE
My favorite character is *Olaf*.
I think *Olaf(he)* is *clever, innocent,*
and *welcoming*.

Disney
FROZEN
Read-Along

초판 발행 2022년 5월 2일

지은이 Disney Press
번역및콘텐츠제작 정소이
영문감수 Julie Tofflemire
편집 정소이 유아름
디자인 박새롬 이순영
저작권 김보경
마케팅 김보미 정경훈

기획 김승규
펴낸이 이수영
펴낸곳 롱테일북스
출판등록 제2015-000191호
주소 04033 서울특별시 마포구 양화로 113(서교동), 3층
전자메일 helper@longtailbooks.co.kr
(학원·학교에서 본도서를 교재로 사용하길 원하시는 경우 전자메일로 문의주시면
자세한 안내를 받으실 수 있습니다.)

ISBN 979-11-91343-38-0 14740

ELSA

ANNA

HANS

KRISTOFF

OLAF

SVEN

Disney
FROZEN

Read Along

Storybook

ISBN 979-11-91343-38-0 14740
Longtail Books

· Storybook ·

When **Princess** Elsa and Princess Anna of Arendelle were little girls, they were the best of friends. Anna was one of the only people who knew Elsa's **secret**: Elsa had the **power** to make snow and ice with just her hands!

One night, Elsa **fill**ed an **empty ballroom** with snow. The sisters played together, building a snowman, **sled**ding, and ice skating.

But as they played, Elsa **lost control.** She **accidentally** hit Anna with a **blast** of icy magic! Anna was **badly** hurt, so her parents went to the **ancient** mountain **troll**s for help. There, a **wise** old troll told them that Anna could be saved—she was lucky to have been hit in the head, not the heart.

Even though Anna **got better**, her parents **worried** that
people would **fear** Elsa's powers. To keep her **gift** a secret, they
surrounded the **castle** with walls and never let anyone inside.
  But whenever Elsa had strong feelings, the magic still **spill**ed
out. Elsa didn't want to hurt her sister again, so she never
played with Anna. That made Anna feel
very lonely.
  Even after their parents were **lost**
in a storm at sea, the sisters didn't
spend any time together.

Years later, it was time for Elsa to become queen of
Arendelle. For just that day, the castle gates were opened!
Hundreds of people **attend**ed the **crown**ing **ceremony**. Elsa
worked hard to hide her feelings—and her powers!

Anna loved meeting all the new people. "I wish it could be
like this all the time."

"Me, too."

At the **coronation** party, Anna danced with **handsome** Prince Hans from the **Southern Isle**s. He made her heart **flutter**. It seemed like they **had** everything **in common**.

Because the gates were just open for one day, Hans and Anna knew this was their only chance to be together. "Can I say something crazy? Will you marry me?"

"Yes!"

Anna and Hans asked Elsa for her **blessing**. But Elsa
thought their **engagement** was a bad idea. "You can't
marry a man you just met. My answer is no."

Anna couldn't believe it. "Why do you **shut** me **out**?
What are you so **afraid** of?"

Elsa started to lose control. "Enough!" As she shouted, ice **shot** from her hands. Everyone **stare**d at Elsa in shock. Now all of Arendelle knew Elsa's secret! Elsa **panic**ked and **fled** for the mountains.

Anna felt **horrible**! Elsa's out-of-control powers had **create**d a **terrible** winter **storm**—in the middle of summer! "I'll bring her back, and I'll make this right." She left Hans **in charge of** the **kingdom**, and **race**d after Elsa on her horse.

But as Anna **rode** through the **fierce** wind, her horse threw her into the snow and ran off back to Arendelle.

Luckily, Anna met an ice **harvester** named Kristoff
and his **reindeer** friend Sven. She asked them for help.
"I know how to stop this winter."
Together, they **set off** to **look for** Elsa.

As they **climb**ed the mountain, Anna and Kristoff **discover**ed
a beautiful winter **wonderland**. There, they met an **enchanted**
snowman named Olaf. Anna thought he looked familiar. "Olaf,
did Elsa build you?"

Olaf smiled. "Yeah. Why?"

"Do you know where she is?"

"Yeah. Why?"

Kristoff **got to the point**. "We need Elsa to bring back summer."

Olaf **was eager to** help them. "Come on!"

Meanwhile, Hans was **hard at work** helping the people of Arendelle. But when Anna's horse came back to the castle **without** her, Hans knew he couldn't stay.

"Princess Anna is in trouble." Hans turned to the **crowd**. "I need **volunteer**s to go with me to find her!" Soon, Hans and some **soldier**s **set out in search of** Anna—and Elsa.

Back on the mountain, Olaf **led** Anna and Kristoff to a
giant ice **palace** that Elsa had created with her powers.
Even Kristoff was **impressed**. "Now that's ice."

Inside, Anna told Elsa about the terrible storm in Arendelle. "It's okay. You can just **unfreeze** it."

Elsa looked worried. "I don't know how."

"That's not good."

Elsa was afraid that if she went back, she would just make the storm **worse**. Arendelle—and Anna—might **be better off** without her. "What am I going to do?"

Anna **tried** over and over again to **convince** Elsa to come home. But Elsa was too **scared** that she would **hurt** more people. As Elsa **argue**d with her sister, an icy **wave** of magic **burst** from her body—and **struck** Anna in the **chest**! "Anna!"

Anna stood up and looked at Elsa. "No. I'm not leaving without you, Elsa."

"Yes, you are." Elsa knew what she had to do.

Elsa used her magic to create a **huge** snowman. He **chase**d the friends **out of** the palace and toward a tall **cliff**.

Kristoff pulled out a rope to help them climb down.

"What if we fall?"

"There's twenty feet of fresh powder down there. It will be like **land**ing on a **pillow** . . . hopefully."

They **leap**ed over the **edge**, and landed safely on the **fluffy** snow below. They had escaped from the snowman, but Anna had other things to worry about. . . .

Anna's hair was turning snowy white!

"It's because she struck you, isn't it?" Kristoff brought Anna to the trolls, hoping they could help. One troll told them that Elsa's icy magic had struck Anna's heart. If the magic was not **reverse**d, Anna would soon be **frozen** solid. Only an act of true love could **thaw** a frozen heart.

Anna knew she loved Hans—maybe a kiss from him would work! As the friends **hurried toward** Arendelle, Anna began to **shiver**. Kristoff was especially worried about her. He was starting to **care for** Anna.

At that moment, Hans and his soldiers had **arrive**d
at the ice palace and **attack**ed Elsa. As she **defend**ed
herself, Elsa **trap**ped one of her attackers behind icy
spikes.

Hans **cried out** to her. "Queen Elsa! Don't be the
monster they fear you are."

Elsa **pause**d, but in her moment of **doubt**, she was **knock**ed **out**. The attackers brought her back to Arendelle and threw her in the **dungeon**.

When Anna arrived in Arendelle, she said good-bye to
Kristoff and Olaf. Then, she raced to see Hans.

As soon as they were alone, Anna asked
Hans to save her with a kiss. But Hans
refused! Anna **realize**d that he had
only **pretend**ed to love her. He
wanted to **take over** Arendelle by
getting **rid of** Anna and Elsa! "All
that's left now is to kill Elsa and bring
back summer."

Hans left Anna alone and shivering. Luckily, Olaf found her and helped her **warm** up by the fire. But Anna was still getting **weak**er and weaker.

As Anna told him about Hans's **evil plan**, Olaf **glance**d out the window and saw Kristoff racing toward the castle. He realized that Kristoff loved Anna. "There's your act of true love right there!" It was Kristoff that Anna needed to kiss! With the last of her **strength**, Anna **struggle**d outside.

Meanwhile, Elsa had **escape**d from the dungeon, but Hans was close behind her. "Elsa, you can't run from this." Hans told Elsa about her magic blast to Anna's heart. "I tried to save her, but it was too late."

Elsa **collapse**d in the snow and closed her eyes. Everything she had done to **protect** her sister had **fail**ed. And it was all her **fault**.

Nearby, Anna was hurrying toward Kristoff when she heard the **clang** of Hans's **sword**. She turned and saw her sister—Elsa was in **danger**!

Instead of saving herself and running to
Kristoff, Anna leaped in front of her sister. "No!"

As Hans **swung** his sword, it **shatter**ed
against Anna's frozen body. She had turned
to **solid** ice.

Elsa **clutch**ed her sister. "Oh, Anna. No. Please, no!" Suddenly, Anna began to thaw! Her arms, warm again, **reach**ed around Elsa, and the two sisters hugged.

As Olaf watched them, he remembered what the wise old troll had said: "An act of true love will thaw a frozen heart." Anna's love for Elsa had saved both of them—and the kingdom.

Soon the two sisters were best friends again, and summer had returned to Arendelle. Elsa even made Olaf a little snow cloud to **keep** him **from melt**ing.

One day, Elsa had a **surprise** for Anna—the castle gates were wide open! "We are never closing them again."

The sisters smiled at each other. Now everything was the way it **was supposed to** be.

Read-Along

An icy adventure!

When the kingdom of Arendelle is trapped
in a never-ending winter, it's up to a fearless
dreamer named Anna to put things right. Anna
teams up with ice harvester Kristoff on an
epic journey to find her sister Elsa, whose icy
powers have caused the terrible storm.